Exploring the Galaxy

Uranus

by Thomas K. Adamson

Consulting Editor: Gail Saunders-Smith, PhD

Consultant: James Gerard
Aerospace Education Specialist, NASA
Kennedy Space Center, Florida

CAPSTONE PRESS
a capstone imprint

Pebble Plus is published by Capstone Press,
151 Good Counsel Drive, P.O. Box 669, Mankato, Minnesota 56002.
www.capstonepub.com

042010
005760

Library of Congress Cataloging-in-Publication Data
Adamson, Thomas K., 1970–
    Uranus / by Thomas K. Adamson.—Rev. and updated.
    p. cm.—(Pebble plus. Exploring the galaxy)
    Includes bibliographical references and index.
    ISBN-13: 978-1-4296-0734-6 (hardcover)
    ISBN-13: 978-1-4296-5815-7 (saddle-stitched)
    1. Uranus (Planet)—Juvenile literature. I. Title. II. Series.
QB681.A33 2008
523.47—dc22
                                        2007004456

Summary: Simple text and photographs describe the planet Uranus.

Editorial Credits
Mari C. Schuh, editor; Kia Adams, designer; Alta Schaffer, photo researcher

Photo Credits
Digital Vision, 5 (Venus)
NASA, 7, 11, 13, 15, 17, 19, 21; JPL, 5 (Jupiter); JPL/Caltech, cover, 1, 5 (Uranus), 9 (Uranus)
PhotoDisc Inc., 4 (Neptune), 5 (Earth, Sun, Mars, Mercury, Saturn), 9 (Earth)

Note: Some of the images in this book are false-color images that use artificial colors to enhance planet features.

Note to Parents and Teachers

The Exploring the Galaxy set supports national science standards related to earth science. This book describes and illustrates the planet Uranus. The photographs support early readers in understanding the text. The repetition of words and phrases helps early readers learn new words. This book also introduces early readers to subject-specific vocabulary words, which are defined in the Glossary section. Early readers may need assistance to read some words and to use the Table of Contents, Glossary, Read More, Internet Sites, and Index sections of the book.

Table of Contents

Uranus

Uranus is the seventh planet from the Sun.

Uranus and the other planets move around the Sun.

The Solar System

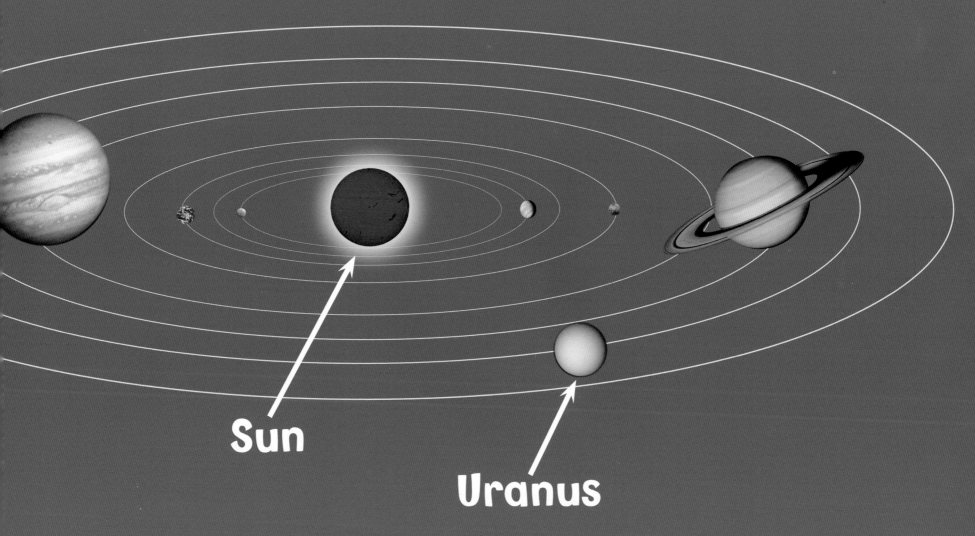

Sun

Uranus

Most planets spin like a top

as they move

around the Sun.

But Uranus spins

on its side.

Uranus is the
third largest planet.
Uranus is four times wider
than Earth.

Earth

Uranus

Moons

At least 21 moons
move around Uranus.
Earth has one moon.

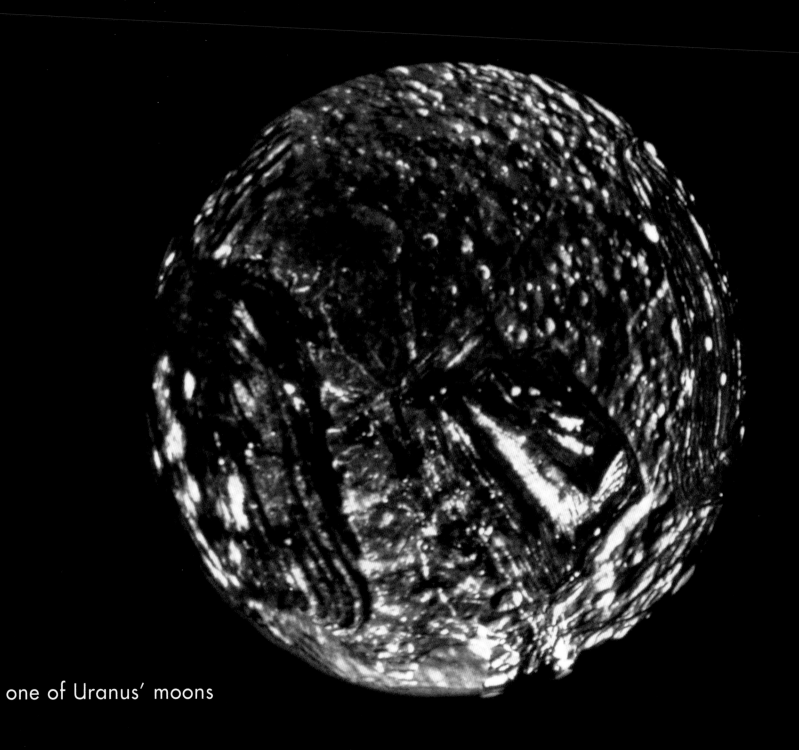

one of Uranus' moons

Features

Uranus is a big ball
of clouds, gases, and liquid.
Uranus is called a gas giant.

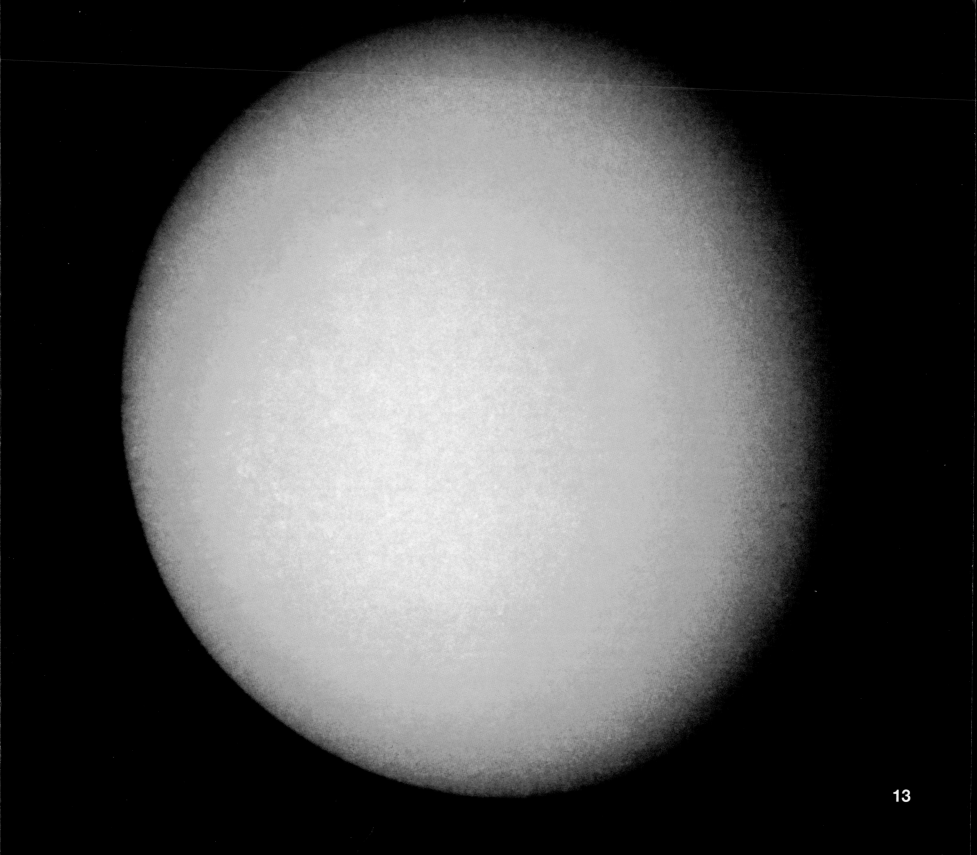

Clouds cover Uranus.

The clouds give Uranus

a blue color.

Uranus has 11 dark rings
around it.
The thin rings are made
of rock and dust.

People and Uranus

Uranus does not have

a solid surface.

A spacecraft could not

land on Uranus.

People could not

walk on Uranus.

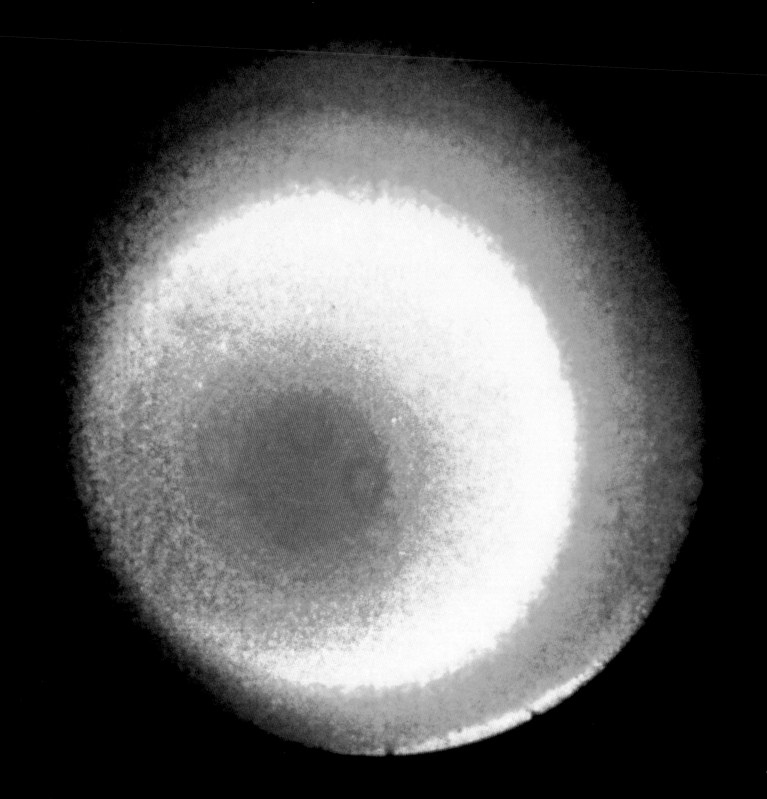

People on Earth cannot
easily see Uranus without
a telescope.
Uranus is too far away.

Glossary

gas—a substance, such as air, that spreads to fill any space that holds it

moon—an object that moves around a planet; Cordelia, Ophelia, Bianca, and Cressida are the moons closest to Uranus.

planet—a large object that moves around the Sun; Uranus is the third largest planet; only Jupiter and Saturn are larger than Uranus; there are eight planets in the solar system.

spacecraft—a vehicle that is used to travel in space

Sun—the star that the planets move around; the Sun provides light and heat for the planets.

surface—the outside or outermost area of something

telescope—a tool people use to look at planets and other objects in space; telescopes make planets and other objects look closer than they really are.

Read More

Adamson, Thomas K. *Uranus.* First Facts: The Solar System. Mankato, Minn.: Capstone Press, 2008.

Bredeson, Carmen. *What is the Solar System?* I Like Space! Berkeley Heights, N.J.: Enslow, 2008.

Wimmer, Teresa. *Uranus.* My First Look at Planets. Mankato, Minn.: Creative Education, 2007.

Internet Sites

FactHound offers a safe, fun way to find Internet sites related to this book. All of the sites on FactHound have been researched by our staff.

Here's how:

1. Visit *www.facthound.com*

2. Choose your grade level.

3. Type in this book ID **9781429607346** for age-appropriate sites. You may also browse subjects by clicking on letters, or by clicking on pictures and words.

4. Click on the **Fetch It** button.

FactHound will fetch the best sites for you!

Index

Word Count: 136
Grade: 1
Early-Intervention Level: 14